CAREER PROFILES™

OPRAH WINFREY

Profile of a Media Mogul

Jeanne Nagle

ROSEN
PUBLISHING®

New York

To Julie, Laura, Mary, Todd, and John for their assistance and support

Published in 2008 by The Rosen Publishing Group, Inc.
29 East 21st Street, New York, NY 10010

Library of Congress Cataloging-in-Publication Data

Nagle, Jeanne M.
Oprah Winfrey : profile of a media mogul / Jeanne Nagle. — 1st ed.
    p. cm. — (Career profiles)
Includes bibliographical references and index.
ISBN-13: 978-1-4042-1908-3
ISBN-10: 1-4042-1908-0
1. Winfrey, Oprah. 2. Television personalities—United States—
Biography. 3. Actors—United States—Biography. I. Title.
PN1992.4.W56N34 2008
791.4502'8092--dc22
[B]

2007001035

Manufactured in Malaysia

C O N T E N T S

Introduction 4

One Growing Up Oprah 8

Two From Troubled to Terrific:
Oprah's Teen Years 23

Three Oprah at Work 36

Four The Turning Point 48

Five Branching Out 63

Six An Influential Woman 80

Timeline 94

Glossary 97

For More Information 100

For Further Reading 103

Bibliography 105

Index 108

INTRODUCTION

When growing up, there are many career choices that capture the imagination. Chances are you have changed your mind about what you want to do plenty of times over the years. That's not unusual. Lots of people have done the same.

That was certainly the case with Oprah Winfrey. As a child, she entertained thoughts of becoming a preacher, a missionary, or a teacher. As a teenager, she thought she might like to be an actress. Curiously, she hadn't considered being a radio announcer or a television newscaster, which are two jobs she wound up holding early in her career. Even

Although she suspected she might do great things, Oprah Winfrey never thought she'd become the glamorous celebrity and media entrepreneur she is today.

working in television, Oprah didn't consider becoming a talk-show host until she found herself on a program called *People Are Talking*.

If she had considered a career in television, Oprah never would have guessed she'd become the huge media entrepreneur she is today. The list of her accomplishments is long. In addition to *The Oprah Winfrey Show*, which has been on the air for almost twenty years, Oprah runs her own company, Harpo Productions, Inc. Through Harpo, she produces television movies and theatrical films (and acts in a number of them), and she creates TV shows such as *Dr. Phil* and *The Rachael Ray Show*. Oprah is also a co-founder of the Oxygen Network, and she publishes a monthly magazine, *O*.

In 2005, Oprah branched out further to become a Broadway producer, helping to stage a musical of the popular movie and novel *The Color Purple*. She also oversees a "women's lifestyle" Web site and recently inked a deal to launch a satellite radio program. As if that weren't enough, Oprah is deeply involved in charitable causes. The Oprah Winfrey Foundation has donated millions of dollars to support nonprofit organizations around the world.

Oprah's career path shows that hard work, discipline, and taking calculated risks will carry you far—maybe farther than you'd ever imagine. Even Oprah's personal life holds many valuable lessons. Hers is a story of faith, of adapting and persevering, of continually learning, and of being aware of what is going on in the world and engaging with it to achieve positive results.

Mostly, though, the story of Oprah Winfrey is a testament to what can happen when you take the time to listen to and care for others, while always remaining true to yourself.

ONE

GROWING UP OPRAH

In Mississippi, about 80 miles (129 kilometers) northeast of the state capital Jackson, there is a town called Kosciusko. In the 1950s, it was a rural community of struggling farms. Today, it is considered one of the nation's best small towns to live in. Kosciusko is now something of a tourist destination, thanks to its most famous former resident, Oprah Winfrey.

Simple Beginning

Oprah Winfrey was born in Kosciusko, Mississippi, on January 29, 1954. Her mother, Vernita Lee, and father, Vernon Winfrey, were never married and did not raise their

The court house in Kosciusko, Mississippi, Oprah's hometown.
Today, Kosciusko is the county seat of Attala County.

daughter together. Instead, Oprah was raised in the house in which she was born—the home of her grandparents, Earlest and Hattie Mae. Her mother lived there, too, for the first few years of Oprah's life, working as a maid to help support the family.

Simple living and hard work were two things Oprah learned early in life. The house in which they lived had no indoor plumbing—the family had to use an outhouse—and they didn't have any other modern conveniences. For instance, Hattie Mae had to boil clothes in a big iron kettle because they didn't have access to a washing machine.

Oprah's grandparents had a tiny plot of land that they farmed. It provided food for the family and not much more. They grew their own produce and raised pigs and chickens. Even as a small girl, Oprah was expected to contribute to the smooth functioning and upkeep of the household. Two of her jobs included feeding the chickens every morning and carrying heavy buckets of well water up to the house.

The rural plot of land where Oprah was raised on her grandparents' farm is now a popular tourist destination.

A Grandmother's Influence

When Oprah was four years old, her mother decided to seek a better life up North. Vernita moved to Milwaukee, Wisconsin, leaving her daughter in the care of the girl's grandparents in Mississippi. Before then, however, Oprah's upbringing had been greatly influenced by her grandmother, Hattie Mae.

A strong, strict woman, Hattie Mae made sure her granddaughter never strayed far from the straight and narrow path. She was not above inflicting physical punishment when Oprah misbehaved, but she was also affectionate. In the introduction to a book written by her hairdresser, Andre Walker, Oprah recalls that one of her happiest childhood memories involves a ritual in which her grandmother would stroke her head while conditioning her hair with oil.

Hattie Mae gave Oprah a precious gift that she cherishes to this day. She taught her to read. She wasn't well educated herself, but Hattie Mae managed to teach Oprah at the age of three how letters were shaped and what sounds they made. This opened up new worlds for her. Oprah has said that, even as a young child, she knew there was more to life than living on a farm, and she had a strong feeling that she could do almost anything she set her mind to. Books introduced Oprah to places and possibilities that were beyond anything she could have imagined.

By teaching her to read and encouraging her to speak at church, Hattie Mae had not only given Oprah important tools that she would use in her eventual career in television—an appreciation and mastery of the written word, experience performing in front of an audience, the ability to communicate well—but also a sense that she could accomplish great things. In many interviews, Oprah has commented on how important an influence her grandmother was on her. In her interview with the Academy of Achievement, Oprah said that living with her grandmother "probably saved my life. It is the reason why I am where I am today. My grandmother gave me the foundation for success that I was allowed to continue to build upon."

The Move North

When she was six years old, Oprah moved to Milwaukee to be with her mother. She went from living in the rural South to a boardinghouse and then an apartment, both in a poor section of a northern, industrialized city. Also, she was no longer an only child. Vernita had given birth to another girl and a son, so Oprah now had half-siblings.

Speaking Up in Church

Hattie Mae was a very religious woman. One of the first books she encouraged Oprah to read was the Bible, and she had the child memorize verses from it. It's no wonder, then, that by the time she was three years old, Oprah had begun reciting Bible verses and giving readings during services at Buffalo Community Methodist Church in Kosciusko. Her first speaking appearance was a retelling of the Easter story. "Other people were known for singing. I was known for talking," she told the Academy of Achievement.

Oprah got lots of attention doing these church recitations. People in the congregation used to tell her grandmother that she was a special child and very bright. Oprah liked hearing that, so she worked hard to prepare and deliver these orations. According to Hattie Mae, Oprah had always been a talker, performing skits and mock interviews on the farm. Now she had a bigger audience that gave her plenty of positive feedback.

Over the years, Oprah's reputation as an orator grew. Throughout her childhood, she continued speaking at churches, reaching beyond Buffalo Community to other congregations. Once, when she was in the third grade, she reportedly received $500 to speak at a church function.

Vernita worked hard as a maid in Milwaukee and didn't always have time to give her daughter attention. For six years Oprah had grown up calling

CAREER PROFILES

Parishioners at Buffalo Community Church were Oprah's first audience. Here she recited Biblical passages as a young girl.

her grandmother "momma." Because she and Vernita had been separated for so long, there was some distance and tension between them. They were no longer familiar with or comfortable around each other.

Oprah turned to some of her oldest friends—books—for comfort. Her mother wasn't much of reader and didn't understand the attraction. She was not as supportive of Oprah being a voracious reader as grandma Hattie Mae had been. In an interview with *Life* magazine in 1997, Oprah recalled an incident in which Vernita ripped a book out of her hands and accused her of thinking she was better than other kids. "I was treated as though something was wrong with me because I wanted to read all the time," she is quoted as saying.

A Gifted Student

One place where Oprah's love of reading was appreciated and encouraged was in school. Building on the promise she showed as an early reader and young orator, Oprah excelled at learning. She was promoted early from kindergarten directly into the first grade, and later she skipped second grade as well.

Oprah was known as a gifted student, meaning she had a higher-than-average intelligence level. She also had a genuine passion for learning. Oprah

Hattie Mae and Earlest Lee raised Oprah until she was six years old. They rest in peace in a Kosciusko cemetery.

attributes this interest in education to the wonderful teachers she had and to the fact that they saw her potential and helped her succeed. One of her favorites was Mrs. Duncan, her fourth-grade teacher. In an interview given to the Academy of Achievement in 1991, Oprah said she was so inspired by Mrs. Duncan that she really started to believe in herself and her abilities. "For the first time, I believed I could do almost anything," she said. "I felt I was the queen bee. I felt I could control the world."

Career Aspirations

During the fourth grade, Oprah began to seriously consider potential career options. Initially, she thought she was destined to become a missionary, envisioning travel to Costa Rica and the sharing of Bible stories with the people there. She has said that she even used to collect money from other children on the school playground to donate to her church's missionary programs.

While at church services, she would listen intently and memorize as much of the pastor's sermon as she could. Then she would go to school on Monday and repeat the sermon during her classroom devotions (moments of prayer or reflection at the beginning of the school day). The other children used to mock her for doing this, calling her "preacher." But she didn't mind. In fact, she thought she might like to become a full-time minister when she grew up.

Another career goal of Oprah's during this time was to become a fourth-grade teacher like her idol, Mrs. Duncan. Years later, in an interview with America Online, Oprah talked about how, if she hadn't become a media celebrity, she would have been just as happy teaching fourth grade. She would have brought the same ambitiousness to the job, claiming she would have been "the greatest fourth-grade teacher and win the Teacher of the Year award."

All these career plans got put on hold, however, on the night of April 13, 1963. That's when a nine-year-old Oprah tuned in to see Sidney Poitier win the Academy Award for his work in "Lilies of the Field." He became the first African American to win an Oscar for Best Actor. The moment made quite an impression on her. As she told Poitier in 2000, "In my spirit I knew that because you had won the

When she saw Sidney Poitier became the first black man to win a Best Actor Oscar, Oprah was inspired to achieve great things in her life.

Oscar, I, too, could do something special—and I didn't even know what it was . . . I thought, 'If he can be that, I wonder what I can be?'" (as quoted in the Academy of Achievement interview).

From then on, Oprah had a new career dream. She had set her sights on becoming an actress.

Wild Child

As well as being a time of intellectual discovery, curiosity, and enthusiasm, fourth grade also marked the start of a tumultuous period in Oprah's life. She has stated that she was molested repeatedly as a young girl—first by a cousin at age nine, and later by friends of her mother and an uncle. Looking back now, Oprah believes that suffering such abuse contributed to how she behaved while living in Milwaukee.

By her own admission, Oprah was rebellious as an adolescent. She frequently lied to her mother, stayed out late, ran away from home, and was sexually promiscuous. "I don't look at my time in Milwaukee with any fondness," she is quoted as saying in a 1998 interview with the *Milwaukee Journal Sentinel*. "I have no regrets about it, but I don't think of it as a fun time. But I think it was necessary because that is what gave me this . . . ambition."

It was Oprah's ambition and potential that caught the eye of teacher Gene Abram, who encouraged her to enroll in Upward Bound, a program that helps prepare low-income students for college. Subsequently, Oprah left Lincoln High School and began attending classes at Nicolet High School in Glendale, an affluent suburb of Milwaukee.

Changing schools didn't help Oprah curb her wild ways much. By all accounts she was popular at Nicolet, but still keenly aware of the differences that existed between her and the other students, chiefly with regard to money. She received a daily reminder that she was poor when she rode to school on a bus with black housekeepers, like her mother, from her neighborhood into Fox Point for work. Most likely, some of them were employed by the wealthy parents of her classmates.

To compensate for this disparity, or gap, between her and her fellow students, Oprah would steal money from her mother. This allowed her to go out and have a good time with her friends, who didn't have to worry about how to pay for things. She also continued to lie to and fight with her mother and get involved with older boys. She was so out of control that Vernita tried to put her into a juvenile detention home. When authorities refused to take the girl because there was no room at the facility, Oprah was sent to live with her father and stepmother in Nashville, Tennessee. As it turns out, that was one of the best things that could have happened to her.

TWO

FROM TROUBLED TO TERRIFIC: OPRAH'S TEEN YEARS

By the time she was fourteen years old, Oprah was, in her own words, headed for a career as a juvenile delinquent. In addition to lying and stealing, she had staged robberies in her Milwaukee home, trying to fool her mother into thinking thieves had taken the items she herself had stolen.

According to her stepsister, Patricia, while their mother was out working, Oprah would invite boys—and sometimes men who were six or seven years older than she—over to the apartment. One of these boys got Oprah pregnant, which she managed to hide from everyone for a long time.

No longer able to handle her daughter, Vernita decided it would be best if Oprah moved in with her father and stepmother in Nashville. The move back to the South occurred in 1968. Within two months Oprah gave birth prematurely to a baby boy, who died shortly after.

While losing the baby was heartbreaking and a terrible shock, Oprah came to see it as a chance to put her troubled past behind her and make a fresh start. That's exactly what living with Vernon and Zelma Winfrey offered her.

Structure and Discipline

Moving to Nashville was a return to the familiar for Oprah in many ways. It wasn't just that the weather was warmer and sunnier, as it had been in her hometown of Kosciusko, Mississippi, or that she was going to be, in effect, an only child again. She was also going to be under the watchful eye of a parental figure who was a demanding disciplinarian.

Vernon was strict, like Grandma Hattie Mae. He strongly believed in discipline and rules. Once in her

Oprah credits her father, Vernon Winfrey, with setting her on the right path and saving her from becoming a juvenile delinquent.

father's home, the unruly child who ran wild in the streets of Milwaukee until all hours now had a curfew. The girl who had been promiscuous was now expected to dress and act like a lady and go on chaste, parentally approved dates.

Just as Hattie Mae had done years earlier, Vernon taught Oprah the value of hard work. This time, however, she wouldn't be feeding chickens or hauling water. In 1970, her father hired her to work in the grocery store he owned and ran. (Vernon also owned and operated a barbershop.) Oprah didn't like the job very much, but she did it because it was expected of her.

Oprah Comes Into Her Own

The structure and discipline Oprah found in her father's home began to yield results within a year or so of her arrival in Tennessee. With her exceptional intelligence and Vernon and Zelma's discipline, Oprah became an honors student at East Nashville High School—an integrated school of middle-class black and white students. She also got involved in extracurricular activities. Oprah was a member of the drama club and was elected class vice president and student council president. In her senior year, she was voted Most Popular Girl by her classmates.

Fostering Oprah's Love of Reading

This belief in hard work most certainly extended to schoolwork as well. Oprah already had proven herself to be a bright and gifted student, and Vernon wouldn't settle for less than her best when it came to grades. She remembers bringing a C home once, and receiving a stern lecture from her father. He told her he wouldn't allow her to bring home anything less than A's because she was an A student. After that, she said to the Academy of Achievement, "I never even tried to bring in a C because I realized that it was just not acceptable."

Like Oprah's mother, Vernon and Zelma were not big readers themselves. Unlike her, though, they encouraged Oprah's reading habit. They wanted to make sure she also appreciated and absorbed everything she read. So, in addition to her schoolwork, Oprah was required to write book reports for her father and stepmother. On top of that, Zelma oversaw vocabulary lessons in which Oprah was required to learn twenty new words a week and use them properly. All the rules and expectations weren't meant to simply raise Oprah's grades. Her father and stepmother also wanted to instill in her a sense of self-worth and pride.

Oprah continued to rack up public speaking engagements. Churches still asked her to come and perform her recitations, which she'd been giving since she was three years old. "I've spoken at every church in Nashville at some point in my life," she

Oprah and Anthony Otey were sweethearts at East Nashville High School. The couple was voted "Most Popular" in their senior year.

said in a 1991 interview with the Academy of Achievement. Her reputation spread beyond the local area. When she was sixteen, she accepted an invitation to speak before a congregation in Los Angeles, California. She frequently spoke before civic groups such as the Elks Club. Her abilities as an orator came in handy when, in 1971, she was selected to represent her high school and the state of Tennessee at the White House Conference on Youth.

Also in 1971, a seventeen-year-old Oprah entered the Miss Fire Prevention contest, representing local radio station WVOL. One of the announcers at the station had interviewed her earlier about a charity event she had participated in and was so impressed by her poise that he suggested the station enter her in the contest on their behalf.

Oprah didn't think she would win, but she figured it would be a fun experience and she would get a new evening gown out of the deal. Because of her low expectations and extensive speaking experience, Oprah was so relaxed in front of the crowd that she had no trouble answering the judges' questions. When they asked what she would do with a million dollars, she replied frankly that she'd "be a spendin' fool," which made everyone laugh.

Then, instead of saying she wanted to be a teacher or an actress when asked what career she wished to pursue, Oprah spontaneously discussed wanting to spread the truth as a television journalist. She had seen Barbara Walters on *The Today Show* (which Walters co-hosted from 1962 to 1976) that morning, and the idea just popped into her head onstage. Despite this very public declaration of her intentions, that was actually the first time Oprah considered a career in broadcasting. Once it occurred to her, however, she was off to the races!

When asked about her future career plans, Oprah told pageant judges she wanted to be a broadcast journalist like Barbara Walters, who, at that time, hosted *The Today Show.*

Hitting the Airwaves

Much to her surprise, Oprah ended up winning the Miss Fire Prevention contest. When she went to the radio station to pick up her prize, they offered her the chance to read news copy and hear what her voice sounded like on tape. Executives at the station were so impressed by how cleanly and clearly she had read the copy that they decided to hire her part time to read the news on the air.

Oprah was still in high school at the time, but she jumped at the chance to work in broadcasting, going into the station after school and on the weekends to read the news. She was used to many people hearing her speak, but this was a bit different. This was her first exposure to the world of broadcast media. In addition to reading, she learned more about the technical aspects of broadcasting and the business end of running a radio station.

The pay wasn't much, but she liked the work. Plus, it meant she didn't have to work in her father's store anymore. She kept the job at WVOL through her graduation from East Nashville High School and into her first few semesters of college.

Off to College

Still determined to be an actress, Oprah enrolled at Tennessee State University in 1971, majoring in dramatic arts and speech communication. She had earned a scholarship to the school after winning yet another beauty and popularity contest, which was sponsored by the local Elks Lodge.

She enjoyed her studies at TSU, was an excellent student, and won parts in school plays. Yet occasionally Oprah struggled to adjust to college life.

For one thing, the 1970s were a time of racial tension and political radicalism in America. Many black students on the TSU campus were extremely militant, meaning they were committed to the struggle against what they viewed as a violent, racist, and unjust white "establishment." While proud of her race and heritage, Oprah did not care to express herself in a politically radical fashion. As she put it in a 1987 interview with *People* magazine, "I refused to conform to the militant thinking of the time."

Instead, she continued to concentrate on her studies, extracurricular activities, the recitations she still gave at churches and other functions, and reading the news at WVOL. It was the last of those activities that would prove to be the most influential stepping stone to her eventual career in broadcasting.

Television Comes Calling

During her sophomore year, a representative of WTVF-TV, the CBS affiliate station in Nashville, heard Oprah on the radio and approached her

Multitalented Oprah Winfrey won a local beauty pageant at the same time she was working for the radio station WVOL, which hired her as a news reader when she was still in high school.

about taking a job in television news. She turned them down three times, afraid that she wouldn't be able to work full time and go to school.

Convinced by a professor that this was a rare and invaluable professional opportunity, Oprah decided to interview at WTVF. She was a little nervous about the meeting because she was familiar with radio, not television. Nevertheless, Oprah got the job. At age nineteen, she had become the youngest—as well as the first black and first female—television news anchor in Nashville history.

Decision Time

Not everyone was happy for Oprah. Her politically militant classmates at TSU accused her of being nothing more than a token, hired by the station because it was required by federal law to include more women and blacks on their staff. Oprah was well aware that part of the reason she was hired at WTVF had something to do with racial and gender quotas. However, she also knew that she was talented. Despite her self-assurance, the opinions and taunts of her TSU classmates began to get to Oprah. She felt unfairly attacked and criticized and became defensive as a result, which made it difficult to enjoy her time in college.

Another challenge Oprah faced was finding the time to do everything she needed to do. Because she was still enrolled at TSU while working at WTVF, Oprah had to keep to a tight schedule. She would take classes from 8 AM until lunch, and then work at the station from 2 PM to 10 PM, including the time she spent on air as the six o'clock news co-anchor. When she got back home, she'd stay awake for hours studying. Then she'd get a little sleep and start the daily cycle all over again.

Eventually the routine got to be too much for Oprah. She had to make a decision: college or a career. She chose to keep her job and drop out of school. Years later she would return and get her degree from TSU, but in 1976, she had left the classroom behind for the newsroom. From then on, there was no looking back. Oprah was starting out on her career as a full-time television personality.

THREE

OPRAH AT WORK

Radio and television are broadcast media, but there are differences in how they operate, as well as what it takes to be successful in them. The most obvious difference is that television is a visual medium. Audiences can see and hear the people reading the news. Although being well groomed and professional in appearance are important, being successful in television news involves more than just how good you look.

Hired as a reporter and co-anchor of the station's weekend newscasts, Oprah was considered on-air talent at WTVF. Her job was to find interesting stories and present them in a concise, accurate, fair, and understandable way to the viewing audience. Beyond that, each of her job titles—anchor and reporter—required additional skills.

News anchors summarize and introduce video-taped news or live transmissions from reporters on the scene. They also read news stories that don't have a video component and are not being reported by someone "on the scene." Some anchors even write their own news copy. The process of anchoring a newscast is like juggling. You must introduce several stories from different sources

Anchoring the news, as Dan Rather used to for the CBS network, requires being able to handle many tasks at once and staying composed while on the air.

quickly and efficiently while working in synch with others in the studio such as a co-anchor, weather and sports anchors, and the many folks behind the scenes who make the broadcast work on a technical level. These include producers, directors, camera operators, and lighting and sound technicians. As you can see, television news is a team effort.

Anchoring is more intricate and involved than simply introducing and reading stories. Among the many skills anchors need to have are the ability to address the camera properly (knowing which of several cameras is on them at any time and speaking to it) and read fluently from a TelePrompter, which is a machine that scrolls text as the anchor reads it.

Similarly, television news reporters are not just on-air personalities who tell stories. They seek out news and follow-up leads, conduct research and interviews, and write copy, which is what the text, or "script," for their stories is called. In smaller markets such as Nashville, reporters edit their own video.

Learning the Ropes

Oprah's talent, intelligence, and dynamic personality were enough to get the attention of the executives at WTVF, secure an interview, and land her the job. She still needed to prove herself in the unknown

The Nature of Television News

Television news is either national, produced directly by the major networks, or local, produced by stations in various cities that are known as affiliates. These affiliates broadcast local news to specific regions of the country called markets, which typically center on a city and its surrounding suburbs. National news focuses on stories of interest to most Americans, while local news tends to concern itself with reporting events that occur within the regional viewing area.

The size of a market is determined by the size of the city and surrounding area that a particular station serves, as well as the size of the area's population of viewers. The three largest markets in the United States are focused around New York City, Los Angeles, and Chicago. As a general rule, the larger the market, the better the pay and the greater the exposure for the on-air talent—those people who work in front of the camera.

environment of a television news studio, though. To do that, she would need to hone the skills she already had acquired and learn new ones.

For one thing, Oprah was in desperate need of a crash course in broadcast journalism. In addition to sitting behind a desk and conveying the news, she was expected to go out on assignment and investigate and film stories. After her years in radio, she could read the news beautifully, but she had never been trained as a reporter.

By her own admission, she was not a strong interviewer at first. "I was more interested in how I phrased the question, how eloquent the question sounded, as opposed to listening to the answer, which always happens when you are interested in impressing people instead of doing what you are supposed to be doing," she told the Academy of Achievement.

Oprah also didn't know how to pull a story together through editing or how to operate the editing equipment. In television, reporters film a bunch of rough video footage at various locations, then take those separate pieces and splice them into a seamless story ready for broadcast by using a video-editing machine. Oprah was at a loss as to how to do any of that.

That's not what she had told the people who

Broadcast reporters go where the news is. They often give taped or live reports from locations outside the television studio, known as "remotes."

hired her, however. "I said I knew how to edit when I didn't," she recalled in her Academy of Achievement interview. "I said I knew how to report on stories . . . I wasn't quite sure of what to do, but I told the news director that I did."

Although confident that she could learn everything she needed to know eventually, Oprah was intimidated by her circumstances. She has said she felt very insecure, as if she was thrown into television without the proper qualifications to handle the job.

Baltimore Comes Calling

With time, determination, and practice, Oprah became good at her job. She had come a long way since her rough start and, little by little, grew into her responsibilities as co-anchor at WTVF. Proof of her improvement is that the station management promoted her to co-anchor of the weeknight newscasts, instead of just the weekend shows. By all accounts, she was popular with audiences in Nashville. They liked the personal touch she brought to the news.

There were other viewers, in a city hundreds of miles away, who also had begun to notice and appreciate the way Oprah was doing her job. In 1976, after spending three years at WTVF, Oprah was approached by representatives of WJZ-TV, the

ABC affiliate and largest station in Baltimore, Maryland. They were looking to add a co-anchor to their soon-to-be-expanded news coverage.

Baltimore was a bigger market than Nashville, so Oprah must have been thrilled by the offer. Just as attractive to her was the opportunity to move out of her father and stepmother's home and strike out on her own. She convinced Vernon and Zelma that moving to Baltimore was good for her career. At age twenty-two, Oprah left to pursue her dreams in a new city.

Changes Afoot

In the space of only five years, Oprah had made her breakthrough in broadcasting at a young age, successfully completed the transition from one medium (radio) to another (television), and was offered a job with a higher salary and greater prestige by a station in a larger market. This fairly quick rise is not how a typical broadcasting career is built, yet it was Oprah's reality. She was beginning to look unstoppable.

Unfortunately, Oprah's news career started to unravel soon after she moved to Baltimore. Actually, there was trouble before she arrived. Some employees of WJZ were not thrilled that Oprah had been offered the co-anchor job. They thought that their co-worker Al Sanders, who hosted a popular Sunday news show, should have been offered the position. Making matters worse, they suspected that Oprah was hired mainly because she was a black woman, and they resented her for it.

Oprah's performance as co-anchor didn't do much to endear her to them. While she had learned a lot about anchoring in Nashville, she was still a little rough around the edges. To begin with, she had problems remaining objective and dispassionate. Journalists are trained to view a story with detachment and just report the facts. Oprah couldn't do that. Her warm, compassionate nature made it impossible for her to report on tragic stories without displaying emotion herself.

Another trouble spot involved what her co-workers saw as unprofessional behavior. Instead of reading copy the way it had been written, Oprah would often ad-lib, putting stories in her own, more casual words. Making matters worse, she and her co-anchor didn't get along very well.

Management at the station quickly realized that Oprah wasn't working out as they had hoped. However, she had signed a multiyear contract, and they couldn't let her go until it expired. Instead, they tried to "fix" her. They paid to have her take lessons

Oprah chats with general manager Jay Newman and former co-host Richard Sher at WJZ 13. The Baltimore television station was where she had her breakthrough as a talk-show host.

with a voice coach and had a famous designer create stylish outfits for her. They also sent her to New York for a makeover, including a French perm that went bad and made her bald.

Her hair grew back after a while, but her self-confidence was completely shaken. "I was devastated because up until that point, I had sort of cruised," she told the Academy of Achievement. "I was twenty-two and embarrassed by the whole thing because I had never failed before."

Management couldn't fire her without breaking her contract, but they could certainly demote her. She was taken off the six o'clock news and given the assignment of anchoring a five-minute early-morning news spot.

A Good Fit

Around this time a new manager at WJZ had an idea that would prove to be Oprah's career salvation. Bill Carter decided the station should produce a morning chat show that focused on local people and events. His plan was to put the program on opposite a show hosted by Phil Donahue, who, at the time, was the reigning king of talk TV. Carter had noticed how Oprah's genuine, empathetic reporting and anchoring style and her way of relating to interview subjects might have no place in a newsroom, but it would be perfect for a talk show. Subsequently, she was hired as the co-host, along

Thanks to her job on *People Are Talking*, Oprah now feels right at home chatting with famous guests like California Gov. Arnold Schwarzenegger and Maria Shriver.

with Richard Sher, of WJZ's new show, *People Are Talking*.

This was where Oprah's "overly emotional" brand of broadcasting would finally come in handy. Unlike what she had experienced with her news co-anchor, she got along well with Sher. They made a great team. She had an easygoing, conversational manner that made people open up to her, and he had an extensive knowledge of Baltimore—its neighborhoods, culture, traditions, and people.

People Are Talking premiered on August 14, 1978. In a 1991 interview with the Academy of Achievement, Oprah recalled the sense of revelation she felt after taping her first hour of the show. "I'll never forget it," she has said. "I came off the air thinking, 'This is what I should have been doing.' Because it was like breathing to me. Like breathing. You just talk. 'Be yourself' is really what I had learned to do."

FOUR

THE TURNING POINT

Oprah Winfrey had found her true calling as co-host of the Baltimore-based morning talk show *People Are Talking*. It became a huge hit that regularly beat Phil Donahue's show in the Baltimore market. It was so popular that WJZ started airing reruns at night. An attempt was made to syndicate the program, which is when an affiliate sells the rights to broadcast a locally produced show to distant markets. WJZ did manage to syndicate *People Are Talking* in a dozen nearby cities, but the show had too much local flavor to be successful outside its original market.

Despite the enormous success of *People Are Talking*, Oprah wasn't completely satisfied with the show and continuously tried to make it better. In a quest to keep things fresh, she moved away from simply doing interviews with local guests who were promoting a product or an event to discussions and examinations of more serious and personal issues. She did this not just to improve the show, but also because the human experience fascinated her and she wanted to learn more about what made people tick. When the show began dedicating a full hour to subjects that touched nearly everyone, like relationships, divorce, families, and depression, ratings went through the roof.

Oprah had hit upon a formula that suited her interviewing style and interests and also resonated with her viewers. *People Are Talking* aired for six years with Oprah as co-host. Then, in 1983, Oprah made a move that would prove to be a turning point in her career—and her life.

A New Home in Chicago

One of the WJZ crewmembers who helped make *People Are Talking* a success was a producer named Debra DeMaio. Producers oversee the entire newscast and are involved in everything from deciding how

Once she had arrived in Chicago, Oprah was so busy she rarely had time to kick back and relax, but once in a while she was able to enjoy the opportunity.

the content of the broadcast will be organized and writing copy, to making sure the on-air talent do their job correctly and checking facts.

Like anyone who hopes to make it big in television, DeMaio was looking to move from Baltimore to a job with a station in one of the top broadcast markets: New York, Los Angeles, or Chicago. She was hired to produce AM *Chicago,* a struggling, half-hour-long, local public affairs program that had lost its host soon after DeMaio came on board. Needing someone she could trust to fill the host slot, DeMaio suggested to the station manager, Dennis Swanson, that he audition Oprah for the position.

For her part, Oprah was excited, though anxious, about the possibility of working in the third-largest television market in the nation. After six years in Baltimore, she had begun to grow restless at WJZ and would welcome the opportunity to further her career by moving into a larger market. Yet despite her success, she had doubts about her abilities. The difficulties of her early days in Baltimore lingered in her mind and still shook her confidence. Also, she had gained weight while in Maryland and was concerned that Chicago audiences would not accept an overweight black woman hosting a show that, up until then, had been led by fit, white men.

The opportunity was too good to pass up, however. Oprah flew to Chicago and auditioned. Swanson had seen a videotape of *People Are Talking* and was impressed, but he remembers being completely blown away by Oprah's live audition at the WLS-TV studios. In an interview with *Broadcasting & Cable* magazine, Swanson recalled a conversation he had with Oprah shortly after she auditioned for him. When she expressed reservations about how the television audience would react to an overweight black woman, he replied, "I am not in the color business.

I am in the win business." He told her he didn't want her to change a thing. He wanted to hire the intelligent, sensational woman who had just auditioned so well. He wanted Oprah just as she was.

At age twenty-nine, she had signed a four-year deal, worth a reported $200,000 a year, with a television station in the third-largest market in the nation. More than that, she had the unwavering support of her producer and the station manager. They shared a belief in her that Oprah had held about herself so many years ago as a child—that she could accomplish great things. Three weeks before her thirtieth birthday, on January 2, 1984, Oprah debuted as co-host of AM *Chicago*.

Turning It Around

DeMaio and Swanson's faith in Oprah turned out to be justified. When she arrived, AM *Chicago* continuously came in last in the ratings for the show's time period. Within only a few months of her arrival, the program had soared to the top of the ratings.

How did Oprah manage this amazing turnaround of AM *Chicago*? A number of factors were involved. First, she got acclimated to her new environment quickly and embraced her new home. Oprah has said that the minute she stepped foot in the streets of Chicago, she felt an immediate bond with the city. She didn't want to be just a guest there, but a full-fledged resident. She did some research, through reading and traveling around, to get to know her new hometown and its residents.

Next, Oprah did her homework. Before interviewing anyone she would find out all she could about the person. That way she would have a thorough knowledge of the guest and could simply have an interesting conversation with the person, rather than a dry, rigid, question-and-answer kind of interview.

Finally, Oprah got to know her "product" and its "consumers"—the show and its viewers. She had watched several segments of AM *Chicago* in preparation for becoming the host. The show was fairly typical of early-morning chat programs of the time, which were aimed at housewives who had just put their kids on the school bus and wanted a little television break before getting on with their day. There was light banter, fashion and cooking tips, maybe some Hollywood gossip, and an occasional celebrity guest. Oprah felt absolutely no connection with this kind of "fluffy" format. That's when she decided to take AM *Chicago* in a new direction.

Breaking New Ground

These days audiences are familiar with a certain kind of talk show, in which a host and guests discuss a particular topic, usually a fairly serious, hard-hitting, socially relevant, or highly personal issue. There is often a certain amount of audience participation, usually in the form of a question-and-answer period. This now-standard, talk-show format was not always the norm, however.

In the 1950s and '60s, there were two basic types of talk shows. News talk programs featured a host with a journalism background who engaged guests in a discussion about current events or politics. There was no studio audience for these types of programs, and viewers tuned in mainly to gain information and be exposed to the ideas and debates that were currently circulating in society and politics. Then there were entertainment-related shows that featured hosts who were often entertainers themselves, like Dinah Shore, Mike Douglas, and Johnny Carson. Their shows featured celebrities who would

Audiences love how Oprah is so down to earth, whether it's sharing her personal struggles or simply being herself in front of the camera.

chat a bit and perform before a live audience. Audience members were exactly that—simply an audience, watching and listening, but not interacting with the host or guests. Viewers (those at home and in the studio) were entertained, but kept at a remove from the action.

All that changed in the 1970s, when the daytime talk show *Donahue* hit the airwaves in Ohio. Former radio and television reporter Phil Donahue pioneered a new type of talk show that blended news with entertainment. Instead of dry news or light entertainment, his shows centered on socially relevant issues that affected everyday people, particularly women, whom he and his producers knew were the bulk of his viewing audience.

Another revolution Donahue introduced to TV talk was audience participation. He left the stage and went into the audience, giving ordinary people a chance to ask a guest questions or make comments on a given topic.

Oprah already had incorporated this "hot topics" brand of TV talk into her show in Baltimore, and it had led to great success. She decided to change the format of AM *Chicago* to reflect this growing trend. She also started going out into the audience with a microphone to capture studio viewers' reactions and

Phil Donahue revolutionized talk television. Using a style similar to his, Oprah managed to beat Donahue regularly in the ratings.

thoughts. She was doing essentially the same thing as Donahue, yet her dynamic personality and intimate, compassionate, and probing interview style gave an extra dimension to her work. She had one big thing in her favor that her competitor could never match— she was Oprah.

Building a Rapport

The same empathetic style that had caused Oprah so many problems as a journalist proved to be her greatest asset as a talk-show host. Guests would feel

Talk Shows Get Trashy

Together, Oprah and Donahue changed the face of talk television. They elevated the format from mere gossip and entertainment to an opportunity to discuss substantial topics of interest to people everywhere. Their success led to the introduction of a slew of journalists, entertainers, and celebrities putting their own shows on the air. Talk shows became like reality shows of the twenty-first century—they flooded the airwaves in the hopes of becoming the next big thing in TV.

Unfortunately, not every host had the talent or integrity of Oprah or Donahue. With fierce competition to attract viewers, new talk-show hosts began to feature segments that were racy and sensational. TV channels suddenly were filled with stories of cheating spouses and medical oddities, strange crime victims and paternity tests. The weirder the topic, the better. The producers of these shows knew that the viewing public would be compelled to watch if only out of curiosity.

Facing a slump in ratings, *The Oprah Winfrey Show* started to discuss issues that were more sensational than serious. The move didn't sit well with her, though, and by 1994 she had made a vow to clean up her program's act. With a renewal to her contract that same year, Oprah also renewed her commitment to the discussion of topics that would uplift and inspire, as well as entertain, her audience.

so comfortable with her that they would forget they were being interviewed and confide in her. Audiences felt like she was a close friend who allowed and encouraged them to discuss matters that had been weighing on their minds.

The fact that she is unafraid to talk about her own troubles makes Oprah more approachable, which makes people feel that they can trust her. As *Chicago* magazine once noted, "No one else on television has been as open as Oprah. Within months of coming to Chicago, she'd told viewers about her troubles with men, [her weight problems], and the terrifying history of her childhood sexual abuse. She told them they could take control of their life energies . . . [and] she gave them the practical means of doing so."

Oprah has said that her ability to get people to open up is based on a "common bond in the human spirit." In other words, she understands people so well because, even though she's a celebrity, she's like them. "We all want the same things, and I know that. . . . And I think people sense that" (as quoted in the Academy of Achievement interview).

The way Oprah conducted herself on air in Chicago set her apart from her main competitor, Phil Donahue. Whereas Donahue was still, in many ways, a reporter, peppering guests with questions, Oprah was having more natural and relaxed conversations with guests. Simply by being herself, Oprah had beaten Donahue at his own game. Within three months, AM *Chicago* was pulling in nearly twice as many viewers as Donahue in the Chicago market. Oprah not only had taken a last-place program and made it into a talk powerhouse, but she had also, as in Baltimore, triumphed over her chief competition. Her ratings victories over Donahue first in Baltimore, then in Chicago, cemented her reputation as a force to be reckoned with in daytime television.

Less than a year after Oprah's arrival, AM *Chicago* was expanded from thirty minutes to an hour-long show. It was also renamed in honor of the driving force that had made it such a huge success. The program was now called *The Oprah Winfrey Show*.

Oprah Goes National

With the show's name change came extra pride in ownership. Oprah became more involved in the running of her show. She was making decisions about which guests to book and what topics would be discussed. Perhaps the smartest decision she made at this time, though, was linking her fortunes with Michael and Roger King of King Brothers Corporation.

In 1984 and 1985, *The Oprah Winfrey Show* was huge in Chicago, but it remained virtually unseen outside of that market. The only exposure folks across

With help from Roger King *(left)* and the blessing of WLS general manager Joseph Ahern, *The Oprah Winfrey Show* was syndicated in 1986.

the United States had to the program was through the reporting on it of the national media. The way the show had taken off so quickly and had consistently beaten Phil Donahue in the local ratings generated coverage in major magazines and newspapers. Oprah also had made an appearance on *The Tonight Show*, formerly hosted by late-night talk-show legend Johnny Carson (though Oprah was interviewed by guest host Joan Rivers).

The media buzz caught the attention of the King brothers, who, after doing a little research, decided they wanted to take Oprah's program to a wider audience. They wanted to syndicate *The Oprah Winfrey Show* nationally.

Syndication involves selling the rights to broadcast shows that are produced by local affiliate stations or any entity that isn't associated with a major network. Syndicators such as the Kings act as agents who convince stations to broadcast shows for a fee. The more popular a show is, the more stations are willing to pay top dollar to air it. A percentage of the sales amount is kept by the syndicators as payment for having made the deal. The bulk of the money, however, goes to the show's creators, which in this case included the program's host and star, Oprah Winfrey.

On September 8, 1986, *The Oprah Winfrey Show* premiered in national syndication, featuring the topic "How to Marry the Man or Woman of Your Choice." Nearly 150 stations had signed on to broadcast the program. The move to syndication had made Oprah incredibly wealthy. In addition, it had introduced her to a much larger audience and made her a popular presence in households across America.

FIVE

BRANCHING OUT

With the syndication of her show, Oprah was quickly becoming one of the hottest commodities in television. It only took about a year before *The Oprah Winfrey Show* had become the top nationally syndicated talk show. In addition to being popular with viewers, the program was well respected by critics and others in the television industry. In just its first year of eligibility, *The Oprah Winfrey Show* won Daytime Emmy awards in three top categories: Outstanding Host, Outstanding Talk/Service Program, and Outstanding Direction.

This kind of astounding success might have satisfied some people

and tempted them to rest on their laurels, but Oprah felt she had much more to give. Known for a strong work ethic and boundless energy, she has taken on a number of different projects and roles over the years, all while maintaining a show that stays at the top of TV ratings.

Since the mid-1980s, Oprah has, among other things, worked as an actress, producer, magazine editor-in-chief, cable network founder, radio broadcaster, and businesswoman. Some of these jobs—such as acting—have represented a realization of her childhood dreams, while others simply show good business sense. Each of them complements and broadens her undisputed reign as "Queen of Talk Television" and "Media Mogul."

Actress

In 1985, at the height of her newfound popularity as a talk-show host in Chicago, Oprah was finally discovered—as an actress. Legendary music producer Quincy Jones was in Chicago on business when he happened to turn on the television and catch

Oprah celebrates a double Daytime Emmy win with boyfriend Stedman Graham.

an episode of Oprah's show. At the time he was writing the music for the film *The Color Purple*, based on the novel of the same name by Alice Walker. When Jones saw Oprah, he became convinced that she would be perfect for the role of Sophia, a strong-spirited woman who endures all that life throws at her with her head held high. At his suggestion, the movie's producers contacted Oprah and invited her to Hollywood for an audition.

Oprah met with director Steven Spielberg and read for the part. According to Oprah biographer and journalist George Mair, Spielberg was astounded by what he saw that day. Once again, Oprah had delivered a killer audition. She was offered the role, beating out several more experienced actresses in the process.

Oprah's landing of a role in *The Color People* illustrates not only the power of positive thinking, but also her firmly held belief that "luck is preparation meeting opportunity." She had been preparing for this big break all her life, with her numerous speaking and public appearances and her drama

As Sofia, on the set of *The Color Purple*, Oprah achieved her dream of becoming an actress with her role in this Steven Spielberg film.

classes at TSU. When Jones and Spielberg offered her the opportunity, she was ready to jump on it.

The director had taken a chance hiring someone who had never had a professional acting job before, but it paid off in a big way. Oprah's performance in *The Color Purple* received both Academy Award and Golden Globe nominations. Since then, Oprah has appeared in other feature films, including *Native Son* and *Beloved*, and a number of television movies.

Producer

While filming *The Color Purple*, Oprah ran into some scheduling difficulties. Shooting the film took months, and management at WLS wasn't happy about parting with the host of their most popular show for so long. Eventually, they reached a compromise, using guest hosts and airing reruns of the show. But the incident made Oprah realize that if she wanted control over her future, she would have to take control of her own show.

In 1986, Oprah formed Harpo Productions. Her new production company took full control and

Beloved was a labor of love for Oprah, who produced and starred in the 1998 film.

became responsible for developing *The Oprah Winfrey Show* two years later. Only the third film and television production studio to be owned by a woman, Harpo (Oprah spelled backward) lets Winfrey handle business arrangements such as financing and promotion, in addition to giving her greater creative control over her show.

Oprah wanted to produce other projects that interested her, no matter what the medium (film, TV, Broadway, print journalism, books, or radio). To reflect that diversity of interests, her company became known as Harpo Entertainment Group, which includes Harpo Productions, Inc.; Harpo Films; Harpo Video, Inc.; and, most recently, Harpo Radio, Inc.

To date, Harpo has developed several movies for television under the banner *Oprah Winfrey Presents* and five television shows. The latter include Oprah's own, as well as *Dr. Phil* and *The Rachael Ray Show*, which are hosted by people who were frequent and popular guests on *The Oprah Winfrey Show*. Harpo's film division was the driving force behind the feature film *Beloved* (based on the novel

After appearing on *The Oprah Winfrey Show* several times as a popular guest, psychologist "Dr. Phil" McGraw started his own daytime talk show, produced by Oprah's Harpo Studios.

by Toni Morrison). It has been tapped to produce *The Great Debaters*, a film starring Denzel Washington that is due to be released in 2008.

Recently Oprah added "Broadway producer" to her resume. In December 2005, a musical version of *The Color Purple* debuted at the Broadway Theatre in New York City. The show was produced by Oprah and Harpo.

When asked why she started her production company, Oprah told the Academy of Achievement that it gave her greater creative and professional control and the freedom to act. But she also has revealed another way that Harpo fits her career goals: "What I really want to do is create films, for myself and for other people, that uplift, enlighten, encourage, and entertain."

Editor-in-Chief

In a meeting with Ellen Levine of the Hearst publication *Good Housekeeping*, Oprah Winfrey was approached about creating a magazine. This wasn't the first time someone had brought up this subject. Oprah had turned down all previous offers, and she had planned to turn this one down as well. She told Levine that her "day job" as talk-show host required a lot of her time, and that she felt her show was already a strong forum for her messages. She said

O: The Oprah Magazine had the most successful launch of any magazine in publishing history.

she couldn't figure out what more a magazine could offer to her audience.

Levine pointed out that the written word was a more permanent record of Oprah's philosophy of living one's best life. The content of a television broadcast may be forgotten within days, but the printed word can be referred back to and read again and again. Oprah told CNN celebrity interviewer Larry King that Levine had added, "We could use this as a personal growth guide . . . a way of executing in print what you try to do every day on your show.' And that was the key for me."

O: The Oprah Magazine hit newsstands in April 2000. It was the most successful magazine launch in publishing history. Building on that success, Oprah began publishing *O at Home* in 2004. Her first magazine was a general women's lifestyle publication, while *O at Home* was to cover home design only.

Cable Network Co-Founder

Continuing her quest to create quality television programming, Oprah invested her money and time in Oxygen Media, which operates cable television's Oxygen Network. Founded in 1998, the network is available in millions of households through local cable providers, DirectTV, and the Dish Network.

Oxygen airs original programming and specials, as well as syndicated reruns that are geared toward women. In addition to reruns of *The Oprah Winfrey Show*, Oxygen carries *Oprah After the Show*, an unscripted half-hour program produced by Harpo, Inc., which shows what happens in the studio after her talk show is taped. It includes extra, previously unaired interview footage with the show's guests.

Back to Radio

Returning to her roots in radio, Oprah signed a deal with XM Satellite Radio. Harpo Radio, a division of Harpo Entertainment Group, produces twenty-four-hour programming for her own channel, XM 156, otherwise known as "Oprah & Friends."

The channel features shows on nutrition, fitness and health, self-improvement, decorating, and current events. A mix of celebrities and everyday people join in conversation with the shows' hosts, all of whom are actually friends of Oprah. Dr. Maya Angelou, designer Nate Berkus, and Oprah's best friend Gayle King are just some of the people who have programs on "Oprah & Friends."

One of Oprah's newest ventures is an XM Satellite radio show, with friends such as fitness expert Bob Greene, poet Maya Angelou, and her real-life best buddy, Gayle King.

Preserving a tradition that began on *The Oprah Winfrey Show,* most of the radio shows feature segments involving audience participation. Listeners call in or send e-mails during the various shows. Oprah herself hosts the weekly call-in show "Talk to Me with Oprah Winfrey." She chats a bit at the beginning of the show to

establish a theme, and callers across the country can phone in with their thoughts on that day's topic or just share a story.

In a press release announcing her affiliation with XM Satellite, Oprah was quoted as saying, "For me, being a part of XM Radio is a full-circle moment because I started out in radio when I was sixteen years old, and now I'm able to share the airwaves with my friends."

Oprah the CEO

Although she claims to not know much about business, Oprah does a good job of making all her enterprises run smoothly. Her success can be attributed to a number of factors.

First, she understands that she is a brand. When people hear the name "Oprah," certain positive associations and phrases come to mind—genuine, charitable, "live your best life." In the business world, this is known as branding—when you associate a high level of value with a product or, in this case, a person.

Many companies have tried to get Oprah to endorse their products and services because they know that having her name associated with something means it will sell very well. She has refused virtually all of these offers. She knows that people trust her to never steer them wrong, and she can't afford to use her name just to make a quick buck. Oprah guards her name, her "brand," carefully.

Second, she pays attention to, and ultimately is responsible for, all business decisions that affect her. She decides which guests and topics will be featured on her show, she reviews every page of *O* before it goes to print, and she personally signs production company checks. Some people might see this as controlling. Oprah sees it as good business sense. As she said to the Academy of Achievement, "One of the . . . big lessons that I've learned, particularly in business, is that you have a responsibility to yourself to learn as much about your business as you can."

Lastly, despite her need for overall control of her growing media empire, Oprah is smart enough to rely on a few trusted advisers. Her syndication partnership with King World is just one example. Also, from the time she started in Chicago, Oprah has worked with lawyer Jeffrey Jacobs. As her business manager and adviser, Jacobs helped her work out the deal with King World and helped her to start her production company.

As she said in her interview with the Academy of Achievement, "I feel best in surroundings where other people are smarter than I am because I feel like I can always learn something from it."

S I X
AN INFLUENTIAL WOMAN

People in the media are in a unique position to influence others. We invite them into our homes every day via the television screen, a radio receiver, the pages of a magazine, or our computer monitors. They become familiar and perhaps trustworthy to us, and we may be impressed and influenced by their glamour and status. Therefore, we often listen to what they have to say.

Because she has so many media forums at her disposal—television, radio, and print—Oprah has been one of the very few people in the entertainment field with the potential to effect genuine and substantial change

President Bill Clinton signs what has become known as "Oprah's Law," which created a database of convicted child abusers.

in our society. Whether it's getting people to read more or encouraging them to give their time and money to those less fortunate, changing the face of talk television or enacting legislation that will protect the nation's children, Oprah has lived up to her reputation as one of *Time* magazine's "Most Influential People."

Oprah's Book Club

Oprah's love of books, which started in her childhood, has only grown through the years. As with

Toni Morrison is just one of many authors whose works have been Oprah's Book Club selections.

everything else she enjoys, she wanted to share the joy of reading with as many people as possible. That led her to form Oprah's Book Club in 1996.

The concept was simple and based on the kinds of book clubs that had been meeting in private homes and bookstores for decades. Oprah would chose a book that she enjoyed reading and announce its title on her show. Viewers were encouraged to go to their neighborhood bookstore to pick up a copy to read themselves. Several weeks later, Oprah would dedicate a show to a thorough discussion of the book. Additional follow-up shows might include a chat with the author, providing readers with interesting background information, such as what or who inspired the book's creation and what the writing process was like, and a more deep and insightful enjoyment of the stories they had read.

From its first installment, the Book Club was a huge success. Estimates put the number of each Oprah's Book Club selection sold at between 600,000 to 1 million. Oprah's viewers were making best sellers of nearly every one of her choices. In fact, *Publisher's Weekly*, a trade journal for the publishing industry, once stated that the only chance a book had of getting on the best-seller lists was to be written by a well-known author or be chosen by Oprah as a Book Club selection. Oprah's Book Club is often credited with helping to prop up the flagging fortunes of the literary fiction publishing industry.

Making readers out of television viewers was not the Book Club's only accomplishment. A number of authors—including Jane Hamilton, Wally Lamb, Janet Fitch, Toni Morrison, and Anita Shreve—were launched or were introduced to a much larger audience because of Oprah's recommendations. Oprah also championed classic works by giants of

American literature such as William Faulkner's *Light in August*, Carson McCullers' *The Heart Is a Lonely Hunter*, and John Steinbeck's *East of Eden*. To show the publishing industry's appreciation for all she has done to encourage reading and the love of books, the National Book Foundation honored Oprah in 1991 with its fiftieth-anniversary gold Medal for Distinguished Contribution to American Letters.

The Spirit of Giving

There is a proverb that says to whom much is given, of him much shall be required. Oprah is a living example of that saying. She became both the first female African American billionaire and the first African American to be named to *Business Week's* list of the most generous philanthropists. Estimates put her charitable giving at $250 million as of 2005. That number has grown considerably since then.

Oprah gives to just about anyone in need, but she does have a few favorite causes. Education, housing, and AIDS awareness and research top her list. Hospitals and arts organizations have benefited from her generosity, too. She contributes heavily to the many charitable initiatives she has established on her own as well. These include the Oprah Winfrey Foundation, the Angel Network, ChristmasKindness South Africa, and the Oprah Winfrey Leadership Academy for Girls.

The Oprah Winfrey Foundation

In 1987, a year after she made a fortune with her show's syndication, Oprah formed the Oprah Winfrey Foundation. According to Oprah.com, the charity was established "to support the inspiration, empowerment, education, and well-being of women, children, and families around the world." Serving as an umbrella organization for her charitable giving, the Oprah Winfrey Foundation has awarded millions of dollars to organizations and projects worldwide that all share the goal of improving education and health care for those in need.

The Angel Network

Such are Oprah's influence and trustworthiness that her viewers tend to respond to her requests enthusiastically and generously. That's definitely the story behind Oprah's Angel Network. What started out as a simple appeal for viewers to donate their spare change in 1998 became an ongoing public charity that, to date, has raised more than $50 million to fund

Artist Amanda Dunbar and singer Charlotte Church make a sizeable donation to Oprah's charitable Angel Network.

nonprofit organizations and various charitable causes.

Oprah's Angel Network was established to give disadvantaged people greater opportunities and to help them fulfill their potential. Funds raised go toward building schools, helping women in war-torn areas become productive citizens, rebuilding communities destroyed by conflict or natural disasters, and much more. The World's Largest Piggy Bank is an Angel Network–funded project aimed at providing scholarships to prospective college students in all fifty states. Another Angel Network campaign, operated in conjunction with Habitat for Humanity, urges people to volunteer their home-building skills in each of the U.S. television markets that carry *The Oprah Winfrey Show*.

Since the Angel Network began, Oprah has covered all

costs associated with running the organization. Subsequently, 100 percent of funds raised can go directly to charity. None of the donations are lost to the paying of administrative costs; Oprah takes care of paying for all of the charity's "overhead."

ChristmasKindness South Africa

In 2004, Oprah, along with a few friends and associates, spent nearly two weeks in South Africa. She visited with children from sixty-three schools in two provinces, getting to know the kids and supplying food, school supplies, and toys. Feeling "transformed" after also visiting orphanages in Africa, Oprah told journalists, "I realized in those moments why I was born, why I am not married and do not have children of my own. These are my children. I made a decision to be a voice for those children, to empower them, to help educate them, so the spirit that burns alive inside each of them does not die" (as quoted in Kyra Kickwood's article "Business Hero: Oprah.").

The South African visit was taped and later aired on *The Oprah Winfrey Show*. During the episode,

Newsweek is among several publications that acknowledge Oprah's position as one of the most influential women in America.

SADDAM IN THE DOCK • A MIERS MELTDOWN?

Newsweek

October 24, 2005 : $3.95

newsweek.msnbc.com

SPECIAL REPORT

How Women Lead

20 of America's Most Powerful Women on Their Lives–And the Lessons They've Learned

Oprah Winfrey, chairman of Harpo Inc.

Oprah made an on-air appeal to her viewers to continue helping the children of South Africa. They wound up donating more than $7 million to the Angel Network, which helped fund a program called ChristmasKindness South Africa. The aim of this program is to support, educate, and uplift South African children whose lives are devastated by AIDS.

Oprah Winfrey's Leadership Academy for Girls

Moved by what she had experienced in South Africa, Oprah decided to help build and staff a school, to be called the Oprah Winfrey Leadership Academy for Girls. Set to open in 2007, the school will train young women to become decision makers and leaders, using advanced education techniques and technology. Teachers and administrators will be selected from among the best of South Africa's educators, and a cutting-edge telecommunications system will allow Oprah herself to teach from Chicago.

The establishment of the Leadership Academy should come as no surprise to anyone who has followed Oprah's career, since she has always placed a great value on schooling. "Education is the way to move mountains, to build bridges, to change the world," she has said on Oprah.com. "Education is the path to the future. I believe that education is indeed freedom. With God's help, these girls will be the future leaders on the path to peace in South Africa and the world."

Career Insight

The strength of Oprah's far-reaching influence can be seen in the number of people who admire her and would like to follow her career path. What might Oprah say to someone asking for career advice?

First, be true to yourself. When the management at WJZ tried to make her over and force her to act more like a traditional, hard-edged, objective journalist, they—and Oprah—failed. It was only when she was allowed to be herself and found the job that fit her personality that she succeeded.

Second, remember Oprah's favorite saying: luck is preparation meeting opportunity. No matter what kind of career you want, you have to practice the skills necessary in your chosen field so you're ready when the opportunity arises.

Third, get a good education and earn the best grades you can. Oprah was fortunate enough to get hired without having finished college, but that's not usually the case for people trying to break into television. Most TV news anchors, especially those who make it into the larger markets, have a college

Thanks to hard work, talent, and the courage to seize opportunities when they arose, Oprah has followed her dreams to lead an amazing life.

degree or some kind of broadcast training, and many talk-show hosts got their start in journalism. Besides, Oprah valued education enough to go back and get her college degree even after she'd tasted career success.

Fourth, be willing to work incredibly hard. Oprah stays busy as much as possible, and she seems to thrive on her hectic schedule. "This is all I do," she once told a reporter. "I do this till I drop. I work on weekends. I go as many places as I can to speak. I get home and I say, 'What am I supposed to do here?'" (as quoted in Janet Lowe's *Oprah Speaks*).

Finally, once your heart is set on a particular career, never give up until you have the job. "You've got to follow your passion," Oprah is quoted as saying by Lowe. "You've got to figure out what it is you love—who you really are. And have the courage to do that. I believe that the only courage anybody ever needs is the courage to follow your own dreams."

1954 Oprah Winfrey is born on January 29 in Kosciusko, Mississippi.

1971 Winfrey is hired to read news in Nashville; named Miss Fire Prevention; enrolls in Tennessee State University.

1973 Winfrey becomes the first African American and youngest co-anchor at WTVF in Nashville.

1976 Winfrey moves to Baltimore to co-anchor the news on WJZ.

1978 Winfrey becomes host of WJZ's show *People Are Talking*.

1984 Winfrey relocates to Chicago for *AM Chicago*; it becomes the No. 1 talk show in Chicago after a month.

1985 *AM Chicago* is renamed *The Oprah Winfrey Show*; Oprah co-stars in *The Color Purple*.

1986 Winfrey founds Harpo, Inc.; her show goes into national syndication.

1991 Winfrey initiates the National Child Protection Act; testifies in the Senate on behalf of the creation of a national database of convicted child abusers.

1993 President Bill Clinton signs "Oprah Bill" into law.

1996 Winfrey launches her book club.

1998 The Angel Network is established; co-founds Oxygen Media; named one of *Time's* "Most Influential People of the Twentieth Century."

2000 Debut of *O: The Oprah Magazine.*

2002 Harpo creates and syndicates *Dr. Phil; Oprah: After the Show* introduced on Oxygen; institutes ChristmasKindness South Africa.

2004 Winfrey begins publication of *O at Home* magazine.

2005 Winfrey again appears on *Time* magazine's list of the "100 Most Influential People"; ranked No. 1 on *Forbes'* Power Celebrity list.

2006 Winfrey signs with XM Satellite to produce "Oprah & Friends" radio show.

GLOSSARY

acclimated To get used to a new situation or environment.

ad-lib To make something up as you go along; to speak spontaneously; to improvise.

affiliate A television station that broadcasts some of its own programming, but also has a connection to the shows produced by one of the major networks.

anchor One who reads the news and presents stories prepared by reporters in the field.

aspiration The hope to achieve a certain goal.

broadcasting Sending out news and entertainment over airwaves via television or radio.

devotions Speaking aloud religious lessons or prayers, performed at church services or similar gatherings.

empathetic Understanding how someone feels because you've felt that way yourself or can imagine feeling that way.

market Specific regions of the country where television and radio programs are broadcast; broadcast markets usually are centered in a city and a wide metropolitan and suburban area surrounding it.

media Used to describe all types of communications that go out to large masses of people; the singular form of media is "medium."

militant Being aggressive, or expressing an idea forcefully.

news copy The text of a story that an anchor or reporter reads.

objective Sticking to the facts; not letting your opinions or emotions get the upper hand.

orator One who is skilled at giving formal speeches.

philanthropy Helping those less fortunate by giving them your time or money.

producer The person who supervises the creation and presentation of a show or similar project.

syndication To sell television affiliates the rights to broadcast a program.

TelePrompter A machine that scrolls the text an anchor, reporter, or actor needs to read aloud.

token Someone hired or allowed into a group merely because of their race, gender, or other characteristics, so that an employer or leader is not accused of discrimination.

tumultuous Difficult, upsetting, unsettled, and confusing.

underserved A person or group of people who do not have the opportunities or status that others have; therefore, their needs do not get much attention, and they don't receive the help they need to keep up with other members of society.

For More Information

Academy of Television Arts and Sciences
5220 Lankershim Boulevard
North Hollywood, CA 91601-3109
(818) 754-2800
Web site: http://www.emmys.org

Canadian Broadcasting Corporation (CBC)
P.O. Box 500, Station A
Toronto, ON, Canada, M5W 1E6
Toll-free (Canada only) (866) 306-4636
Web site: http://www.cbc.ca

Harpo Productions, Inc.
110 North Carpenter Street
Chicago, IL 60607-2146
(312) 633-1000
Web site: http://www.oprah.com

King World Productions
2401 Colorado Avenue, Suite 110
Santa Monica, CA 90404
(310) 264-3300
E-mail: contactus@kingworld.com

Museum of Television and Radio East
25 West 52nd Street
New York, NY 10019
(212) 621-6800
Web site: http://www.mtr.org

Museum of Television and Radio West
465 North Beverly Drive
Beverly Hills, CA 90210
(310) 786-1025
Web site: http://www.mtr.org

O Magazine and *O at Home*
300 West 57th Street
New York, NY 10019-5915
(212) 903-5366
Web site: http://www.hearstcorp.com/
magazines/property/mag_prop_o_2000.html

Oprah's Angel Network
P.O. Box 96600
Chicago, IL 60693
Web site: http://www.oprah.com/uyl/
oan_landing.jhtml

Oxygen Media, LLC
75 9th Avenue

New York, NY 10011

Web site: http://www.oxygen.com

XM Satellite Radio

1500 Eckington Place NE

Washington, DC 20002

(202) 380-4000

Web site: http://www.xmradio.com

XM Satellite Radio (Canada)

175 Avenue Road

Toronto, Ontario M5R 2J2

(877) 438-9677

Web site: http://www.xmradio.ca

Web Sites

Due to the changing nature of Internet links, the Rosen Publishing Group, Inc., has developed an online list of Web sites related to the subject of this book. This site is updated regularly. Please use this link to access the list:

http://www.rosenlinks.com/cp/opwi

FOR FURTHER READING

Ali, Dominic, and Michael Cho. *Media Madness: An Insider's Guide to Media*. Tonawanda, NY: Kids Can Press, Ltd., 2005.

Englart, Mindi. *How Do I Become a . . . TV Reporter?* Chicago, IL: Blackbirch Press/Thomson Gale, 2003.

Garson, Helen S. *Oprah Winfrey: A Biography*. Westport, CT: Greenwood Press, 2004.

Holland, Gini. *Oprah Winfrey: An Unauthorized Biography*. Chicago, IL: Heinemann Library, 2001.

Krohn, Katherine E. *Oprah Winfrey* (Just the Facts Biographies). Minneapolis, MN: Lerner Publishing Group, 2004.

Nagle, Jeanne. *Careers in Television*. New York, NY: The Rosen Publishing Group, 2001.

Paprocki, Sherry. *Oprah Winfrey: Talk Show Host and Media Magnate*. New York, NY: Chelsea House, 2006.

Seguin, James. *Media Career Guide: Preparing for Jobs in the 21st Century*. New York, NY: Bedford/St. Martin's, 2005.

Westen, Robin. *Oprah Winfrey: "I Don't Believe in Failure."* Berkeley Heights, NJ: Enslow Publishers, Inc., 2005.

Various/Inc. *Facts on File. Discovering Careers for Your Future: Radio and Television.* New York, NY: Ferguson Publishing Co., 2005.

BIBLIOGRAPHY

AOL. Interview with Oprah Winfrey. October 3, 1995.

Cleadge, Pearl. "Walking in the light—interview with Oprah Winfrey." *Essence*. June 1991.

Dudek, Duane. "Oprah is author of her own success." *Milwaukee Journal Sentinel* Online. Oct. 11, 1998. Retrieved November 5, 2006 (www2.jsonline.com/letsgo/movies/1011oprah.stm).

Froeklke Coburn, Marcia. "Doyenne of Dish." *Chicago Magazine*, March 1992, p. 82.

Garson, Helen S. *Oprah Winfrey: A Biography.* Westport, CT: Greenwood Press, 2004.

Greene, Bob, and Oprah Winfrey. *Make the Connection: Ten Steps to a Better Body and a Better Life.* New York, NY: Hyperion/Harpo, Inc., 1996.

Johnson, Marilyn, and Dana Fineman. "Oprah Winfrey: A Life in Books. *Life*. September 1997, p.9.

Kirkwood, Kyra. "Business Hero: Oprah." MyHero.com. Retrieved January 2007 (http://www.myhero.com/myhero/hero.asp?hero=oprahhero).

Lawrence, Ken. *The World According to Oprah: An Unauthorized Portrait in Her Own Words.* Kansas

City, MO: Andrews McMeel Publishing, 2005.

Lowe, Janet. *Oprah Winfrey Speaks: Insight from the World's Most Influential Voice.* New York, NY: John Wiley & Sons, Inc., 1998.

Mair, George. *Oprah Winfrey: The Real Story.* Secaucus, NJ: Birch Lane Press, 1994.

Nagle, Jeanne. *Careers in Television.* New York, NY: The Rosen Publishing Group, 2001.

"Oprah Winfrey Interview." AcademyOfAchievement. org. Feb. 21, 1991. Retrieved October 2006 (http://www.achievement.org/autodoc/page/win0int-1).

Paul, Franklin. "Oprah Winfrey Set to Debut Channel on XM Satellite." Yahoo! News. Sept. 22, 2006. Retrieved Oct. 16, 2006 (http://ca.news.yahoo.com/s/22092006/6/n-entertainment-oprah-winfrey-set-debut-channel-xm-satellite.html).

Perkins, Ken Parish. "Long journey to the top." SpokesmanReview.com. May 9, 2004. Retrieved Nov. 1, 2006 (www.spokesmanreview.com/pf.asp?date=050904&ID=s1517831).

Poitier, Sidney. "Oprah Winfrey: Talk Show Inspiration." *Time* Online. April 26, 2004. Retrieved Oct. 16, 2006 (http://www.time.com/time/magazine/printout/0,8816,994053,00.html).

Richman, Alan. "Oprah." *People Weekly*. January 12,

1987, p.56.

Romano, Allison. "Hall of Fame: Dennis Swanson." Broadcasting & Cable.com. Oct. 24, 2005. Retrieved Nov. 17, 2006 (http://www. broadcastingcable.com/article/CA6276873. html?display=Hall+of+Fame).

Sellers, Patricia. "The Business of Being Oprah." Mutual of America/*Fortune* Online. April 1, 2002. Retrieved Nov. 19, 2006 (http://www. mutualofamerica.com/articles/Fortune/ 2002_04_08/Oprah1.asp).

Tannen, Deborah. "The *Time* 100: Artists and Entertainers." *Time* Online. 2003. Retrieved Nov. 5, 2006 (http://www.time.com/time/ time100/artists/profile/winfrey.html).

INDEX

A

Academy of Achievement, 12,
    13, 17, 20, 27, 28, 40, 41,
    45, 47, 59, 72, 79
Academy Award, 18, 68
AM Chicago, 50, 52–53, 56,
    59, 60
America Online, 18
The Angel Network, 85, 87–88
Angelou, Maya, 75

B

Baltimore (Md.), 42, 48, 50,
    51, 60
Beloved, 68, 70–71
Berkus, Nate, 75
Broadcasting & Cable
    magazine, 51
Buffalo Community Methodist
    Church, 13
Business Week magazine, 84

C

Carson, Johnny, 55, 61
Chicago (Ill.), 50, 51, 53, 59, 60,
    65, 79, 90
Chicago magazine, 59
ChristmasKindness South Africa,
    88, 90
CNN, 74
The Color Purple, 6, 67–68, 72

D

Daytime Emmy award, 63
DeMaio, Debra, 49, 50, 52
DirectTV, 75
Dish Network, 75
Donahue, 56
Donahue, Phil, 46, 48,56, 57,
    58, 59, 60, 61
Douglas, Mike, 55
Dr. Phil, 6, 70

E

East of Eden, 84
East Nashville High School,
    26, 31
Elks Club, 28
Elks Lodge, 31

F

Faulkner, William, 84
Fitch, Janet, 83

G

Golden Globes, 68
Good Housekeeping magazine, 72
The Great Debaters, 72

H

Habitat for Humanity, 87
Hamilton, Jane, 83

Harpo Entertainment Group, 70, 75
Harpo Films, 70
Harpo Productions, Inc., 6, 68, 70, 72, 75
Harpo Radio, Inc., 70, 75
Harpo Video, Inc., 70
Hearst Publications, 72
The Heart Is a Lonely Hunter, 84

J

Jacobs, Jeffrey, 79
Jones, Quincy, 65, 67

K

King Brothers Corporation, 69
King, Gayle, 75
King, Larry, 74
King World, 79
Kosciusko (Miss.), 8, 13, 25

L

Lamb, Wally, 83
Lee, Earlest (grandfather), 9
Lee, Hattie Mae (grandmother), 9, 11–12, 13, 15, 25, 26
Lee, Vernita (mother), 8, 11, 12, 13, 14, 15, 21, 25
Levine, Ellen, 72, 74
Life magazine, 15
Light in August, 84
"Lilies of the Field," 18
Lincoln High School (Milwaukee), 21
Lowe, Janet, 93

M

McCullers, Carson, 84
Medal for Distinguished Contribution to American Letters, 84
Milwaukee (Wis.), 11–12, 20, 23
Milwaukee Journal Sentinel, 20
Miss Fire Prevention contest, 28–30
Morrison, Toni, 72, 83

N

Nashville (Tenn.), 22, 25, 26, 27, 31, 38, 41, 42
National Book Foundation, 84
Native Son, 68
Nicolet High School (Milwaukee), 21

O

O At Home, 74
O: The Oprah Magazine, 6, 72, 74, 78
"Oprah & Friends," 75
Oprah After the Show, 75
Oprah's Book Club, 81–84
Oprah.com, 85, 90
Oprah Speaks, 93
The Oprah Winfrey Foundation, 6, 85
Oprah Winfrey Leadership Academy for Girls, 90–91
Oprah Winfrey Presents, 70
The Oprah Winfrey Show
  mission of, 58
  offshoots of, 6, 70

origin of, 60
ratings slump, 58
reruns of, 68, 75
success of, 6, 63, 65
syndication of, 62, 63, 85, 87
Oscar (award), 18, 20
Oxygen Media, 74
Oxygen Network, 6, 74, 75

P

People Are Talking, 6, 47,
    48–49, 51
People magazine, 32
Poitier, Sidney, 18
Publisher's Weekly trade
    journal, 83

R

The Rachel Ray Show, 6, 70
Rivers, Joan, 61

S

Shore, Dinah, 55
Shreve, Anita, 83
Spielberg, Steven, 67, 68
Steinbeck, John, 84

T

"Talk to Me with Oprah
    Winfrey," 76
TelePrompter, 38
Tennessee State University
    (TSU), 31, 32, 34,
    35, 68
Time magazine, 81

The Today Show, 29
The Tonight Show, 61

U

Upward Bound, 21

W

Walker, Alice, 67
Walker, Andre (hairdresser), 11
Walters, Barbara, 29
Washington, Denzel, 72
White House Conference on
    Youth, 28
Winfrey, Oprah
    academic achievement,
        16–17, 26, 27, 31
    as actress, 65, 67–68
    as cable network co-founder,
        6, 70, 74–75
    as CEO, 78–79
    and charitable causes, 6, 29,
        84–85, 87–88, 90–91
    and church, 4, 12, 13, 17–18,
        27–28
    and college life, 31–32,
        34–35, 93
    early ambitions, 4, 17–18,
        20, 29, 65
    as the first female African
        American billionaire, 84
    growing up in Kosciusko,
        8–12
    growing up in Milwaukee,
        12–13, 15–18, 20–23
    growing up in Nashville, 22,
        25–32

half-siblings of, 12, 23
her name as a "brand," 78
influence of father on, 26
influence of grandmother
    on, 11, 12, 13, 26
influence of teachers on, 17,
    18, 21
love of reading, 11–12, 15,
    16, 27, 70, 81–84
as magazine co-founder, 6,
    65, 70, 72, 74
as morning talk-show host,
    45–49, 51–53, 56–62
philosophy of "living one's
    best life," 74, 78
as producer, 6, 65, 68, 70, 72
as "Queen of Talk
    Television," 65
radio broadcasting career of,
    30–31, 32, 34, 42
on satellite radio, 6, 65, 70,
    75–77
saying of "Luck is preparation
    meeting opportunity,"
    67, 91
and sexual abuse, 20, 59
style as a talk-show host, 46,
    47, 53, 57–60

television news career of,
    5–6, 32, 34,
    36–37, 38–43,
    45–47
tension with mother, 15, 20,
    21–23, 25
as a troubled teen, 20,
    21–23, 25
and weight problems, 51, 59
Winfrey, Vernon (father), 8,
    25–27, 42
Winfrey, Zelma (stepmother),
    25, 26, 27, 42
WJZ-TV television station, 41,
    42, 45, 47, 48, 49,
    51, 91
WLS-TV television station,
    51, 68
The World's Largest Piggy
    Bank, 87
WTVF-TV television station, 32,
    34, 35, 36, 38, 41
WVOL radio station, 29,
    31, 32

X

XM Radio, 77
XM Satellite Radio, 75, 77

About the Author

Training and experience as a journalist have given Jeanne Nagle an insider's perspective on the media and what it takes to succeed in this field. The author of several books, including *Rosen's Careers in Television*, Nagle also has worked as a reporter, film critic, and managing editor of the television and movie section of a weekly newspaper. Her extensive research has led to a heightened interest in the power of broadcasting, as well as a greater appreciation of Oprah Winfrey's personal character, business sense, and professional resolve.

Photo Credits